SARA JOINS
THE CIRCUS

Written by Thera S. Callahan
Illustrated by Chum McLeod

Children's Press®
A Division of Scholastic Inc.
New York • Toronto • London • Auckland • Sydney
Mexico City • New Delhi • Hong Kong
Danbury, Connecticut

For Katie and Claire
—T. S. C.

Reading Consultants

Linda Cornwell
Literacy Specialist

Katharine A. Kane
Education Consultant
(Retired, San Diego County Office of Education
and San Diego State University)

Library of Congress Cataloging-in-Publication Data

Callahan, Thera S.
   Sara joins the circus / written by Thera S. Callahan; illustrated
by Chum McLeod.
       p. cm. — (Rookie reader)
       Summary: Sara wants to join the circus so she practices and
prepares and, after many weeks, she takes her show on the road.
       ISBN 0-516-22273-2 (lib. bdg.)   0-516-27384-1 (pbk.)
       [1. Circus — Fiction.] I. McLeod, Chum, ill. II. Title. III. Series.
PZ7.C12975 Sar 2002
[E] — dc21

                                          2001003834

Sara wanted to join the circus.

But first,
she would need to practice.

For weeks she juggled,

balanced,

trained animals,

clowned around,

walked on her hands,

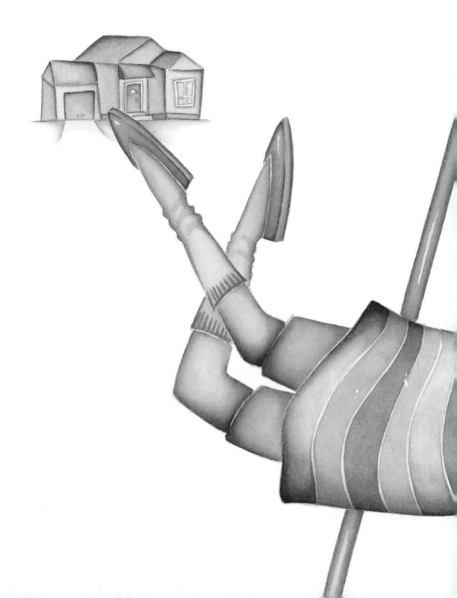

twirled in the air,

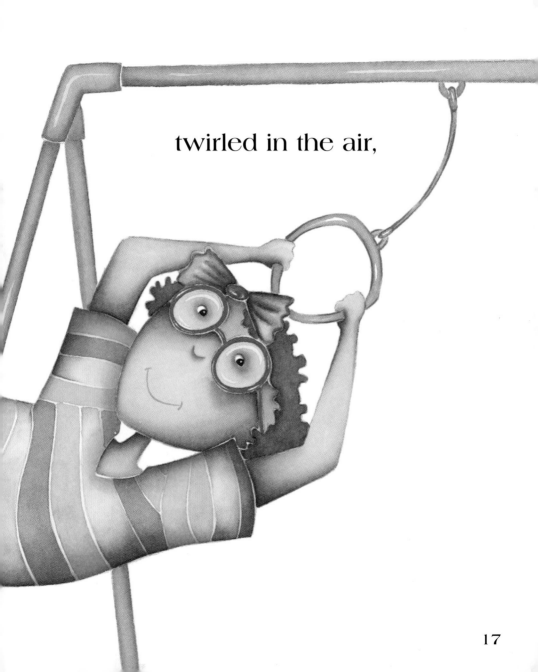

flipped upside down,

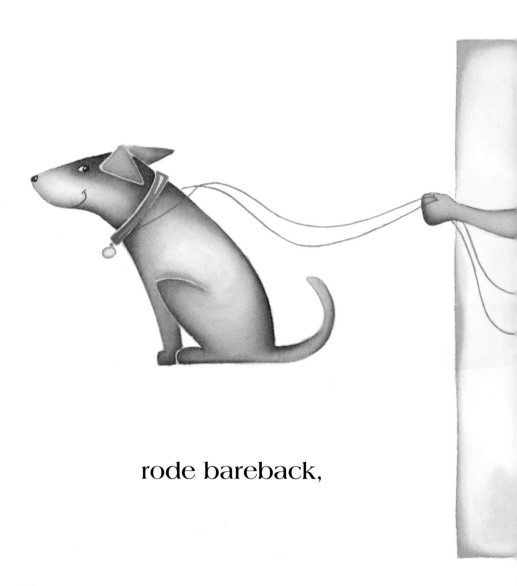

rode bareback,

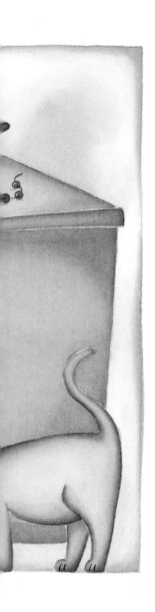

made costumes,

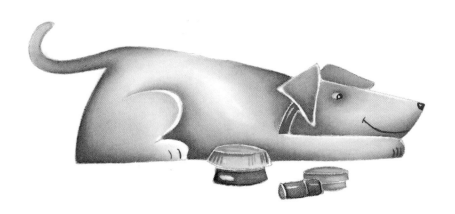

tried on makeup,

and painted posters.

Finally,
Sara was ready to take
her show on the road.
Well . . .

. . . as far as the driveway.

Word List (50 words)

air	for	Sara
and	hands	she
animals	her	show
around	in	take
as	join	the
balanced	joins	to
bareback	juggled	trained
but	made	tried
circus	makeup	twirled
clowned	need	upside
costumes	on	walked
down	painted	wanted
driveway	posters	was
far	practice	weeks
finally	ready	well
first	road	would
flipped	rode	

About the Author

Thera Callahan retired from a career in healthcare administration five years ago to spend more time with her family, renovate an 1860s farmhouse, and write children's books. This addition to the Rookie Reader series is her first publication. She lives in Philadelphia with her husband, Clark, and their two daughters, Katie and Claire. Thera and her entire family enjoy going to the circus. Katie and Claire's dreams of performing center ring were inspiration for this book.

About the Illustrator

When Chum was young she *really* wanted to join the circus. Instead, she went to art school and became an illustrator. She loves drawing and painting and has illustrated more than twenty books. She is still trying to learn how to juggle.